CONTENTS

IT'S A DRAGON!

Two villagers are travelling in the mountains thousands of years ago. They discover some dinosaur bones. But they don't know what kind of beast the bones are from. One of the villagers cries, "It must be a dragon!"

DRAGON FACT

Ancient people did not know much about animals and nature. They often made up stories about dragons or other monsters to explain what they saw.

When ancient people saw dinosaur **fossils**, their imaginations probably ran wild. Today's dragon **myths** may have grown from the stories told by these frightened people.

fossil remains or traces of an animal or a plant, preserved as rock

myth story told long ago that many people believed to be true

Today we know dragons aren't real. But some real-life beasts look like dragons. The bones of prehistoric animals and some current animal **species** remind us of dragons.

species group of animals with similar features

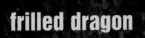

frilled dragon

PREHISTORIC MONSTERS

Dinosaurs are easy to mistake for dragons. *Tyrannosaurus rex* was one of the largest **predators** of all time. This huge beast grew up to 6 metres (20 feet) tall. It also had 18-centimetre (7-inch) teeth.

predator animal that hunts other animals for food

DRAGON FACT

The name *Tyrannosaurus rex* means "king tyrant lizard".

Pterosaurs were large flying **reptiles** that lived with the dinosaurs. Some had **wingspans** up to 12 metres (40 feet). Most had long, narrow heads and small, sharp teeth.

reptile cold-blooded animal that breathes air and has a backbone

wingspan distance between the tips of a pair of wings when fully open

DRAGON FACT

Dragons in most stories also have large wings and sharp teeth.

13

LIVING LEGENDS

Dinosaurs died out millions of years ago. Yet stories about dragons are found in **cultures** all over the world. Could some prehistoric creatures have survived into recent times? If so, people might have mistaken such animals for dragons.

culture people's way of life, ideas, customs, and traditions

Loch Ness monster

DRAGON FACT

The coelacanth is an ancient fish that was once thought to have died out. But several have been found since 1938. Perhaps ancient sailors thought this large fish was a sea dragon.

plesiosaur

People have reported seeing Scotland's Loch Ness monster for hundreds of years. There is no proof that the creature is real. But it may have led to some old dragon legends from Scotland.

DRAGON FACT

Plesiosaurs were large swimming reptiles. They lived alongside the dinosaurs. Some people think the Loch Ness monster might be a surviving plesiosaur.

oarfish

Ancient sailors often told stories about their lives at sea. They didn't know much about ocean animals such as oarfish or giant squid. People may have thought these creatures were huge sea dragons.

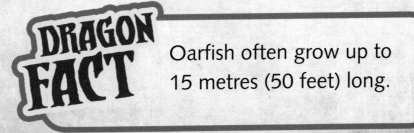

DRAGON FACT Oarfish often grow up to 15 metres (50 feet) long.

TODAY'S DRAGON-LIKE CREATURES

Several modern animals remind people of dragons. Alligators and crocodiles have long jaws filled with jagged teeth. They also have long tails and thick, armour-like skin.

Chinese alligators have long, thin bodies. They look very similar to pictures of dragons from China and Japan.

American alligator

21

About 50 kinds of deadly bacteria live in the mouth of a Komodo dragon.

Komodo dragons are the largest lizards in the world. They have sharp claws, razor-sharp teeth, and a **venomous** bite. Komodos can easily remind people of fierce dragons.

venomous having or producing a poison called venom

23

Giant Pacific salamanders have long, flexible bodies and tough skin. Some Asian dragon stories may be based on these animals.

Some sea creatures look like dragons. Leafy sea dragons get their name from their dragon-like appearance. Dragon moray eels have mouths full of sharp teeth.

dragon moray eel

The sky is also filled with animals that have dragon-like features. People may think of dragons when they see large vultures soar overhead. Large dragonflies may also bring dragons to people's minds.

DRAGON FACT

Some large dragonflies fly faster than 32 kilometres (20 miles) per hour.

bearded dragon

DRAGON FACT

Some dragon-like animals are kept as pets. Lizards such as frilled dragons and bearded dragons are popular pets.

People have told dragon stories for thousands of years. Dragons aren't real, but people still enjoy imagining them. Everywhere people look, real creatures remind them of fire-breathing dragons.

GLOSSARY

bacteria very small living things that exist all around you and inside you; some bacteria cause disease

culture people's way of life, ideas, customs, and traditions

fossil remains or traces of an animal or a plant, preserved as rock

myth story told long ago that many people believed to be true

plesiosaur large swimming reptile that lived during the time of the dinosaurs

predator animal that hunts other animals for food

reptile cold-blooded animal that breathes air and has a backbone; most reptiles lay eggs and have scaly skin

species group of animals with similar features

venomous having or producing a poison called venom

wingspan distance between the tips of a pair of wings when fully open

READ MORE

Non-fiction

How to Draw Dragons, Mark Bergin (Bookhouse, 2010)

Fiction

Dragon Rider, Cornelia Funke (Chicken House, 2005)

Dragonblood series, Michael Dahl (Raintree, 2010)

No Such Thing as Dragons, Philip Reeve (Marion Lloyd Books, 2010)

The Hobbit, J.R.R. Tolkien (HarperCollins, 2012)

WEBITES

FactHound offers a safe, fun way to find websites related to this book. All the sites on FactHound have been researched by our staff.

Here's all you do:

Visit *www.facthound.com*

Type in this code: 9781406266610

INDEX